S0-BAR-649

H♥W T♥ MAKE L♥VE T♥ A CAT

by Hodge

PRODUCED BY
PHILIP LIEF

ILLUSTRATED BY
Jeff Danziger

CORNERSTONE LIBRARY
Published by Simon & Schuster
NEW YORK

OTHER BOOKS BY HODGE
CAT'S REVENGE
CAT'S REVENGE II
MORE CAT TALES, STARRING HODGE

Copyright © 1982 by Philip Lief

All rights reserved
including the right of reproduction
in whole or in part in any form

Published by CORNERSTONE LIBRARY,
A Simon & Schuster Division of
Gulf & Western Corporation
Simon & Schuster Building
1230 Avenue of the Americas
New York, New York 10020

CORNERSTONE LIBRARY and colophon are
trademarks of Simon & Schuster,
registered in the U.S. Patent and
Trademark Office.

10 9 8 7 6 5 4 3 2 1

ISBN 0-346-12563-4

Not long ago, a feline-fancying friend came to me with a problem. She had just acquired a new cat. He was a big, handsome Russian Blue, and she loved him to distraction. But he treated her like a dog.

"What am I going to do, Hodge?" my friend moaned. "I'm simply wild about this cat, but he doesn't seem to give a meow about me."

I proceeded to give her a few simple pointers about how to please even the most truculent of Toms, and she departed, greatly relieved.

In the days that followed, this conversation preyed on my mind. It occurred to me that there were probably plenty of other ailurophiles like my friend who could benefit from my intimate knowledge of the feline heart. So, once again I took pen in paw to write a book I knew would revolutionize the relationship between *Homo Sapiens* and *Felis Domestica.*

In preparing HOW TO MAKE LOVE TO A CAT, I naturally drew heavily upon my own experience. But I also interviewed hundreds of cats from all walks of life — from fat cats to hepcats, from social lions to 'fraidy cats. Then I set down my findings in simple cat-to-person language.

Cat lovers, rejoice! Here is the book you've been waiting for — the ultimate answer to the question: "What Do Cats Really Want?"

Hodge

FETCHINGLY

Your cat will appreciate proof of doglike devotion.

MONUMENTALLY

Commission a sculptor to render your cat's likeness in stone.

AROMATICALLY

**Promise her anything,
but give her Chatte No. 5.**

COSMICALLY

Persuade Carl Sagan to name a constellation after her.

MAGNANIMOUSLY

Buy him a mouse ranch in Montana.

GASTRONOMICALLY

The cat is a born gourmet. Caviar is better for courtship than kibble.

GLAMOROUSLY

Nothing becomes a legend more.

TRADITIONALLY

Find her father and ask for her paw.

CINEMATICALLY

Make her a star.

CHASTELY

Most cats appreciate being chased. In fact, you cannot make love to one until you catch it.

DESIGNINGLY

Cats look great in Calvins.

CATNIPTIOUSLY

Let her grow her own.

GARFIENDISHLY

**A big plate of pasta has been known
to make some pussies passionate.**

TOMFOOLISHLY

**Spend Saturday mornings together watching
"Tom and Jerry" re-runs.**

ROMANTICALLY

Play the balcony scene from "Romeo and Juliet."

DIMINUTIVELY

**Try shrinking down to your cat's size, but watch out.
If you become so small the cat wonders if you are a man
or a mouse, no amount of squeaking will save you.**

LITTERALLY

**Cats hate to run out of necessaries.
Keep her well-supplied.**

Sentimentally

Court him with flowers and boxes of chocolate-coated mousies.

BARNSTORMILY

Let your cat pretend to be the Red Baron.
You can pretend to have nine lives.

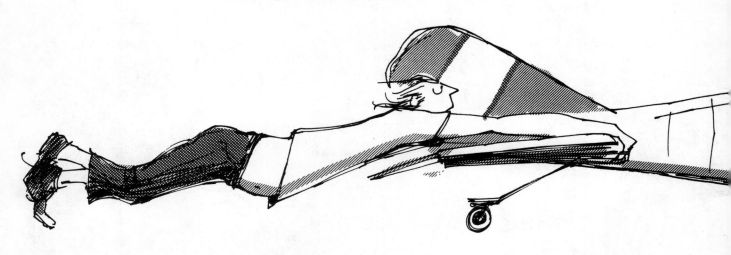

ETERNALLY

Reserve a place for her in your family plot.

OBSEQUIOUSLY

**Think of yourself as a lowly peasant
and your cat as the lordly Shogun.**

LONG-WINDEDLY

**Read to your cat from The Congressional Record.
After a few hours, she will be putty in your hands.**

CAGILY

If you make love to the Big Cats, one or the other of you had better be in a cage.

IMPRESSIVELY

Roll out the red carpet for her.

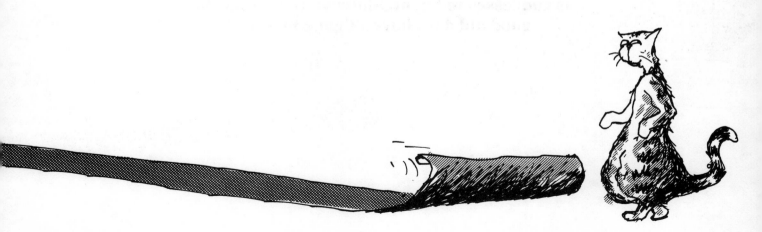

DIVINELY

Cats are nostalgic for the era when they were worshipped as goddesses in Egypt. Show your cat that the good old days haven't gone forever.

LUCKILY

Take your cat to Las Vegas and let him play his hunches.

IDOLATROUSLY

People like to be worshipped, but cats expect it. A full-scale replica of Easter Island in feline motif will create a favorable environment for backyard lovemaking.

SUPERFLUOUSLY

Your cat will enjoy going shopping with you, provided he gets to fill the cart.

SOAP-OPERATICALLY

**Some cats are born performers. If your feline
has such a flair, she will appreciate a part
in one of the daytime dramas.**

PRIMITIVELY

Play Tarzan to her Jane.

BLINDLY

On the third day of Christmas, give him a trio of mice.

FEUDALLY

Be her Knight in Shining Armor.

THOUGHTFULLY

**After a hard night's hunting, your cat
will enjoy breakfast in bed.**

PISCATORIALLY

**Cats are great lovers of seafood.
Make Friday "fresh catch" day.**

SLAVISHLY

The cat is the creature-comfort creature par excellence, and will be delighted with the attentions of a harem slave.

CAVALIERLY

**To be as gallant as Sir Walter Raleigh,
offer the cat your hat as a litterbox.**

CLOWNISHLY

It is difficult to make love to a bored cat,
so engage a troupe of clowns to amuse her.

MAGICALLY

Show your cat that you have a few tricks up your sleeve.

UPROARIOUSLY

Cats like having company, so allow your feline to invite a few friends over while you're away.

EXPENSIVELY

Diamonds are a cat's best friend.

DAREDEVILISHLY

Arouse you cat's interest with a few simple stunts.

GINGERLY

Make love to your cat the way Fred Astaire made love to Ginger Rogers.

GRANDLY

When they must travel, cats like to do so in style.
Hire a gondola for her next trip to the vet.

PRIVATELY

What you and your cat do is your own business.

WILLINGLY

Leave it all to her.

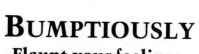

BUMPTIOUSLY
**Flaunt your feelings
with a bumper sticker.**

I ♥ MY CAT